M000302381

PEARSON

my World

Social Studies®

Here We Are

PEARSON

Boston, Massachusetts
Chandler, Arizona
Glenview, Illinois
New York, New York

Illustrations Front Cover, **119** Rick Whipple; Back Cover, **54, 55, 58** Aga Kowalska; **6, 22, 23, 32, 35, 36** Holli Conger; **7, 59, 124, 125** Carlos Aon; **12, 13, 43, 72, 73, 84, 103** Shirley Beckes; **14, 15** Paul Eric Roca; **17, 79, 102** Steffane McClary; **20, 107** Gwen Keraval; **31, 71** Nancy Davis; **38, 110, 111** Bob Barner; **44, 90, 94, 96** Marion Billett; **52** Karen Roy; **53, 92** Viviana Garafoli; **60, 61, 69** Lyn Boyer; **66, 71** Ivanke & Lola; **75** Allegra Agliardi; **80, 93** Laura Huliska-Beith; **82** Louise Ellis; **97, 98** Kory Heinzen; **106** Jenny Matheson.

Maps XNR Productions

Photographs Every effort has been made to secure permission and provide appropriate credit for photographic material. The publisher deeply regrets any omission and pledges to correct errors called to its attention in subsequent editions.

Unless otherwise acknowledged, all photographs are the property of Pearson Education, Inc.

Photo locators denoted as follows: Top (T), Center (C), Bottom (B), Left (L), Right (R), Background (Bkgd)

Text CVR1 (TL) Albert de Bruijn, 2010/Shutterstock, (C) Ariel Skelley/Getty Images, (CR) Hemera/Thinkstock, (BL) Spass/Shutterstock, (BL) Per-Anders Pettersson/Contributor/Getty Images News/Getty Images, (T) Susan Montgomery, 2010/Shutterstock, (BC) United States Mint; **CVR2** (TR) ©DK Images, (BL) Paper Boat Creative/Getty Images, (CC) Tom Tracy Photography/Alamy Images; **1** (Bkgrd) Ariel Skelley/Getty Images; **2** (CR) iStockphoto/Thinkstock, (TR, CR, BR) Pearson; **4** (CL) Cynthia Farmer/Shutterstock, (BL) Bob Daemmrich/Alamy Images, (TR) Jupiterimages/Thinkstock, (BR) Thinkstock; **5** (L) Ariel Skelley/Getty Images; **6** (TL) Ariel Skelley /Getty Images, (BR) JLP/Jose L. Pelaez/Corbis, (BL) Jupiterimages /Thinkstock, (TR) MaszaS/Shutterstock; **13** (R) Andersen Ross/Blend Images/Getty Images, (L) Brand X Pictures/Thinkstock, (C) Plus69/Shutterstock; **15** (R) Creasource/Corbis, (L) Shutterstock; **21** (R) Goodshoot/Thinkstock, (C) Jupiterimages/Photos/Thinkstock, (L) Susan Montgomery, 2010/Shutterstock; **22** (TL) ©DK Images, (BR) KLAUS NIGGE/National Geographic Image Collection, (TC) Richard Fitzer/Shutterstock, (TR) Stockbyte/Thinkstock, (BL) Susan Montgomery, 2010/Shutterstock; **23** (BL) LWPhotography/Shutterstock, (TL) Thinkstock, (R) Tom Brakefield/Stockbyte/Thinkstock; **24** (BR) Albert de Bruijn, 2010/Shutterstock, (TC) Michael Felix Photography/Shutterstock, (BL) Rafal Olechowski/Shutterstock; **27** (Bkgrd) Ariel Skelley/Blend Images/Getty Images; **28** (TR, CR, BR) Pearson; **30** (BL) ©DK Images, (TL) Amanda Flagg, 2010/Shutterstock, (CL) Hemera/Thinkstock, (CR) iStockphoto/Thinkstock, (BR) Jose Inc/Blend Images/Photolibrary Group, Inc., (TR) Ikonoklast Fotografie/Shutterstock; **31** (CL, BR) ©DK Images, (CR) Anetta, 2010/Shutterstock, (CR) DK Images, (C) iStockphoto/Thinkstock; **32** (TL) Galushko Sergey/Shutterstock, (TR) iStockphoto/Thinkstock, (BR) Petrenko Andriy, 2010/Shutterstock, (BL) Roman Sigaev/Shutterstock; **35** (L) ©DK Images, (R) SW Productions/Getty Images; **37** (Bkgrd) BananaStock/Thinkstock; **39** (R) Joe Sohm/Visions of America, LLC/Alamy, (C) Hill Street Studios/Blend Images/Getty Images, (L) Kraig Scarbinsky/Getty Images; **40** (BC) Brand X Pictures/Thinkstock, (TL) Africa Studio/Fotolia, (TC) mangostock, 2010/Shutterstock, (BR) Thinkstock, (BL) Thomas M Perkins/Shutterstock, (TR) Tom Tracy Photography/Alamy Images; **43** (TL) Coprid/Shutterstock, (TR, BC) Hemera/Thinkstock; **44** (BR) Digifoto Neptune/Alamy, (BL) Hemera/Thinkstock, (TR) Jupiterimages/Thinkstock, (TL) Stockbyte/Thinkstock; **45** (R) Blend Images/Alamy, (L) moodboard/Photolibrary Group, Inc.; **46** (R) Blend Images/DreamPictures/Getty Images, (CL) Comstock/Thinkstock, (CR) Ikonoklast Fotografie/Shutterstock, (L) Ragnar Schmuck/fStop/Photolibrary Group, Inc.; **49** (Bkgrd) Ariel Skelley/Getty Images; **50** (TR, CR, BR) Pearson; **52** (CL) ©Jupiterimages/Thinkstock, (TR) Aurora Photos/Alamy, (BL) Jupiterimages/Thinkstock, (CR) Kevin Fleming/Corbis, (TL) Per-Anders Pettersson/Contributor/Getty Images News/Getty Images, (BR) spacephotos com/AGE Fotostock; **54** (BR) iStockphoto/Thinkstock, (BC) studiots/Shutterstock, (BL) Thinkstock; **56** (C) iStockphoto/Thinkstock, (TR) Aurora Photos/Alamy, (BR) Hemera Technologies/Photos/Thinkstock, (TL) Photos/Thinkstock; **63** (TL) Kevin Fleming/Corbis, (BR) Sensi Images/Alamy Images, (CR) spacephotos com/AGE Fotostock; **66** (BR) ©DK Images, (TR) Aurora Photos/Alamy, (TL) Sensi Images/Alamy Images, (BL)

Thinkstock; **67** (C) JLP/Jose L. Pelaez/Corbis; **69** (CL) Jupiterimages/Getty Images//Thinkstock, (C) Steve Skjold/Alamy Images, (R) Stockbyte/Getty Images; **73** (C) ©Charlie Waite/Getty Images, (CL) Alan Novelli/Alamy Images, (BR) robyelo357/Fotolia, (TR) John W Banagan/Iconica/Getty Images, (BC) Spyros Bourboulis/First Light/Corbis, (BL) Wally Stemberger, 2010/Shutterstock; **77** (Bkgrd) Justin Guariglia/Getty Images; **78** (TR, CR, BR) Pearson; **80** (BR) Asia Images/Getty Images, (TL) Bill Bachmann/Alamy Images, (BL) Blend Images/SuperStock, (TR) Morgan Lane Photography/Alamy, (CR) Phil Date, 2010/Shutterstock, (CL) Thinkstock; **83** (R) BananaStock/Thinkstock, (L) moodboard/Corbis; **85** (BR) Golden Pixels LLC/Alamy, (C, BL) Monkey Business Images, 2010/Shutterstock, (TR) Ocean/Corbis, (TL) Jupiterimages/Thinkstock; **87** (TR) Blend Images/SuperStock, (BL) MARK RALSTON/AFP/Getty Images, (BR) Ryan McVay/Getty Images, (TL) Stewart Cohen/Pam Ostrow/Blend Images/Getty Images; **89** (R) BananaStock/Thinkstock, (L) Brand X Pictures/Jupiterimages/Thinkstock, (C) Thinkstock; **91** (C) Ariel Skelley/Photographer's Choice/Getty Images, (C) Blend Images/SuperStock, (CR) gary718, 2009/Shutterstock, (L) JP Laffont/Sygma/Corbis; **95** (BR) adam eastland/Alamy Images, (TL) Blend Images/Patrik Giardino/Getty Images, (BL) frans lemmens/Alamy Images, (TR) Paul Barton/Corbis; **101** (C) H. Armstrong Roberts/Retrofile/Getty Images, (L) Jupiterimages/Comstock/Thinkstock, (R) Jupiterimages/Thinkstock; **102** (TR, CR, BR) Pearson; **104** (CR) ©Associated Press, (BR) ©Kenneth Sponsier/Shutterstock, (CL) Andre Adams/Shutterstock, (BL) Cameilia, 2010/Shutterstock, (TR) George Marks/Retrofile/Getty Images, (TL) JGI/Jamie Grill/Blend Images//Corbis; **105** (CL) Gelpi/Shutterstock, (CR) iStockphoto/Thinkstock, (R) Photodisc/Getty Images/Thinkstock, (L) Ryan McVay/The Image Bank/Getty Images; **106** (BC) Anetta, 2010/Shutterstock, (R) Hemera/Thinkstock, (TC) iStockphoto/Thinkstock, (L) Vereshchagin Dmitry/Shutterstock; **111** (R) JGI/Blend Images/Corbis, (L) Thinkstock; **113** (C) Hemera/Thinkstock, (R) iStockphoto/Thinkstock, (L) Ljupco Smokovski, 2010/Shutterstock; **114** (R) BananaStock/Thinkstock, (L) Tony Campbell, 2010/Shutterstock, (C) Tony Campbell/Shutterstock; **115** (L) Image Source/Getty Images, (TR) Images/Alamy Images, (BR) Thinkstock; **116** (L) Comstock/Getty Images, (R) frescomovie, 2010/Shutterstock, (C) Hemera/Thinkstock; **117** (Bkgrd) Ariel Skelley/Getty Images; **118** (L) Denis Felix/Taxi/Getty Images, (C) Gary S Chapman/Stone/Getty Images; **119** (R) ©Associated Press, (C) DK Images, (L) INTERFOTO/Alamy Images; **121** (L) George Marks/Retrofile/Getty Images, (R) Image Source/Getty Images; **122** (BR) ©DK Images, (BL) Comstock/Thinkstock, (TR) Hemera/Thinkstock, (TL, CL) iStockphoto/Thinkstock; **123** (R) Hemera/Thinkstock, (L) SuperStock/Getty Images; **124** (BR) Hemera/Thinkstock, (TR) IStockphoto/Thinkstock, (TL) iStockphoto/Thinkstock, (BL) LAMB/Alamy; **127** (R) Bambu Productions/Iconica/Getty Images, (L) Evening Standard/Hulton Archive/Getty Images; **128** (TL) ©DK Images, (CL) Carlos E. Santa Maria, 2009/Shutterstock, (CR) David Brimm, 2010/Shutterstock, (BR) ene, 2009/Shutterstock, (BL) Hemera Technologies/PhotoObjects/Thinkstock, (TR) iStockphoto/Thinkstock.

Copyright © 2013 Pearson Education, Inc., or its affiliates. All Rights Reserved. Printed in the United States of America. This publication is protected by copyright, and permission should be obtained from the publisher prior to any prohibited reproduction, storage in a retrieval system, or transmission in any form or by any means, electronic, mechanical, photocopying, recording, or otherwise. For information regarding permissions, request forms, and the appropriate contacts within the Pearson Education Global Rights & Permissions department, please visit www.pearsoned.com/permissions/.

PEARSON, ALWAYS LEARNING, and myWorld Social Studies are exclusive trademarks owned by Pearson Education, Inc. or its affiliates in the U.S. and/or other countries.

PEARSON

ISBN-13: 978-0-328-70337-1
ISBN-10: 0-328-70337-0

20   18

Program Consulting Authors

The Colonial Williamsburg Foundation
Williamsburg, Virginia

Dr. Linda Bennett
Associate Professor,
Department of Learning,
Teaching, & Curriculum
College of Education
University of Missouri
Columbia, MO

Dr. Jim Cummins
Professor of Curriculum,
Teaching, and Learning
Ontario Institute for
Studies in Education
University of Toronto
Toronto, Ontario

Dr. James B. Kracht
Byrne Chair for Student
Success
Executive Associate Dean
College of Education and
Human Development
Texas A&M University
College Station, Texas

Dr. Alfred Tatum
Associate Professor,
Director of the UIC
Reading Clinic
Literacy, Language, and
Culture Program
University of Illinois at
Chicago
Chicago, Illinois

Dr. William E. White
Vice President for
Productions, Publications
and Learning Ventures
The Colonial Williamsburg
Foundation
Williamsburg, VA

Consultants and Reviewers

PROGRAM CONSULTANT

Dr. Grant Wiggins
Coauthor, *Understanding by Design*

ACADEMIC REVIEWERS

Bob Sandman
Adjunct Assistant
Professor of Business and
Economics
Wilmington College–
Cincinnati Branches
Blue Ash, OH

Jeanette Menendez
Reading Coach
Doral Academy
Elementary
Miami, FL

Kathy T. Glass
Author, *Lesson Design for
Differentiated Instruction*
President, Glass
Educational Consulting
Woodside, CA

Roberta Logan
African Studies Specialist
Retired, Boston Public
Schools/Mission Hill
School
Boston, MA

**PROGRAM TEACHER
REVIEWERS**

Andrea Baerwald
Boise, ID

Riley D. Browning
Gilbert Middle School
Gilbert, WV

Charity L. Carr
Stroudsburg Area School
District
Stroudsburg, PA

**Stacy Ann Figueroa,
M.B.A.**
Wyndham Lakes
Elementary
Orlando, FL

LaBrenica Harris
John Herbert Phillips
Academy
Birmingham, AL

Marianne Mack
Union Ridge Elementary
Ridgefield, WA

Emily L. Manigault
Richland School District #2
Columbia, SC

Marybeth A. McGuire
Warwick School
Department
Warwick, RI

Laura Pahr
Holmes Elementary
Chicago, IL

Jennifer Palmer
Shady Hills Elementary
Spring Hill, FL

Claire Riddell
Jacksonville, FL

Diana E. Rizo
Miami-Dade County
Public Schools
Miami Dade College
Miami, FL

Kyle Roach
Amherst Elementary,
Knox County Schools
Knoxville, TN

Eretta Rose
MacMillan Elementary
School
Montgomery, AL

Nancy Thornblad
Millard Public Schools
Omaha, NE

Jennifer Transue
Siegfried Elementary
Northampton, PA

Dennise G. Zobel
Pittsford Schools-Allen
Creek
Rochester, NY

My Family, My School

THE BIG ? How do people best cooperate?

Copyright © Pearson Education, Inc., or its affiliates. All Rights Reserved.

Teaching Note: Explain that *cooperate* means to "work together." Discuss how the children in the photo work together to carry the large American flag. Ask what might happen if the children in the photo did not cooperate or work together well.

My Family, My School

Draw a picture of yourself working with a friend.

Copyright © Pearson Education, Inc., or its affiliates. All Rights Reserved.

Teaching Note: Discuss ways children can work together to do a school project or a classroom job. Use the photos on the page for ideas. Then read the prompt aloud. Ask the child to describe the picture he or she drew of working with a friend.

♫ Begin With a Song

We Go to School

Sing to the tune of "The Farmer in the Dell."

We go to school each day.

We learn in every way.

We learn to read

And write and spell.

We learn to work and play.

Copyright © Pearson Education, Inc., or its affiliates. All Rights Reserved.

Teaching Note: Sing the song as you point to the picture that goes with each part. Then have the child point to the pictures as you both sing the song again.

Ask what other activities he or she learns and does in school each day.

Vocabulary Preview

Circle examples of these words in the picture.

citizen

school

leader

FRANKLIN SCHOOL

rule

symbol

monument

Copyright © Pearson Education, Inc., or its affiliates. All Rights Reserved.

Teaching Note: Point to the small photos as you read the words aloud. Use additional examples to define each word. Then tour the central picture with the child and discuss the scene. Say each vocabulary word and assist the child in circling an example in the picture.

What makes a good citizen?

I can help. I can take turns.

Copyright © Pearson Education, Inc., or its affiliates. All Rights Reserved.

Teaching Note: Use the photos and the text to help the child understand what makes a good citizen. Then brainstorm additional ideas for how children can help, take turns, and show that they are good citizens.

What makes a good citizen?

Tell how these children are good citizens.

Copyright © Pearson Education, Inc., or its affiliates. All Rights Reserved.

Teaching Note: Read the prompt aloud. Discuss different ways that people can be good citizens. Talk about how the people in the photos are good citizens. Then have the child tell an additional example of how he or she can be a good citizen.

What are rights? What are responsibilities?

I live in a home.
I help my family.

I go to school.
I listen to my teacher.

Copyright © Pearson Education, Inc., or its affiliates. All Rights Reserved.

Teaching Note: Use the text to help the child understand the meaning of *rights*. Explain that children have the right to a home and to go to school. Do the same for *responsibilities*. Discuss what it means to help your family and listen to teachers.

What are rights? What are responsibilities?

Draw pictures. Show how you help.

Home

School

Copyright © Pearson Education, Inc., or its affiliates. All Rights Reserved.

Teaching Note: Read the prompt. Brainstorm with the child ways he or she helps at home and at school. Write down the answers and read them together. Then have the child draw how he or she helps at school and at home and describe the final picture.

Copyright © Pearson Education, Inc., or its affiliates. All Rights Reserved.

Lesson 3

How do we get along with others?

Look at the children at the swing. What is the problem?

How did they solve the problem?

Teaching Note: Cover the picture on the right. Then point to the left picture and ask what the problem is. Talk about how the girls could solve their problem. Uncover the right picture and discuss how the girls are sharing the swing and taking turns.

9

How do we get along with others?

Look at the children at school.
Tell about the problem.

Draw a picture to solve the problem.

Copyright © Pearson Education, Inc., or its affiliates. All Rights Reserved.

Teaching Note: Read the prompts to the child and talk about the problem in the picture. Then have the child draw a picture that shows how the problem might be solved. Ask the child to describe his or her solution.

Reading Skills: Main Idea and Details

The main idea tells what a story is about. The details tell more about the main idea.

<u>Anna and Ben go to school.</u>

They help each other read.

They share toys.

They clean up, too.

main idea

detail

detail

detail

Copyright © Pearson Education, Inc., or its affiliates. All Rights Reserved.

Teaching Note: Read aloud the text. Discuss how the picture labeled "Main Idea" illustrates the underlined sentence. Then reread each sentence, and have the child point to the picture that shows the detail of what Anna and Ben do in school.

© **RI.K.2.** Identify main topic and retell key details.

Reading Skills: Main Idea and Details

Try it!

Underline the main idea.

Lin takes care of Barker.

She gives him a bath.

She feeds him.

Lin takes Barker for a walk, too.

Write "d" under the details.

main idea

Copyright © Pearson Education, Inc., or its affiliates. All Rights Reserved.

Teaching Note: Read the story aloud. Have the child underline the main idea. Then ask the child to look at each picture and write a "d" under it to indicate that the picture shows a detail that supports the main idea of what Lin does to take care of Barker. Read each sentence and have the child point to the corresponding picture.

What rules do we follow?

Good citizens follow rules.

home

school

community

Copyright © Pearson Education, Inc., or its affiliates. All Rights Reserved.

Teaching Note: Discuss the meaning of *rules*. Then ask the child to give an example of a rule at home, in school, and in the community. Use the photos to encourage ideas. Then talk about why following rules is something a good citizen does.

What rules do we follow?

Circle people who follow rules.

Copyright © Pearson Education, Inc., or its affiliates. All Rights Reserved.

Teaching Note: Ask the child what he or she sees in the picture. Then talk about what each person in the picture is doing. Read the prompt and help the child circle the people who are following rules. Have the child point to people who are not following rules.

Copyright © Pearson Education, Inc., or its affiliates. All Rights Reserved.

Lesson 5

Who are our leaders?

Leaders help us in many ways.

Teaching Note: Talk about the photos. Then ask how a parent is helping as a leader in the left photo and how the firefighter is helping as a leader in the right photo.

Brainstorm rules and laws the leaders are helping the children learn.

15

Who are our leaders?

Name a leader. **Tell** how the leader helps us.

Copyright © Pearson Education, Inc., or its affiliates. All Rights Reserved.

Teaching Note: Assist the child in naming the leader in each photo as a teacher, a doctor or nurse, a librarian, and a crossing guard. Discuss how each leader may help children follow rules and obey laws.

How do we make decisions?

We make decisions in many ways.

Copyright © Pearson Education, Inc., or its affiliates. All Rights Reserved.

Teaching Note: Define *decision* as a choice made from two or more things such as activities. Use the illustrations to brainstorm ways people can make decisions together, such as voting and talking about ideas. Help the child identify additional ways to make decisions.

How do we make decisions?

Draw one way you make a decision with friends.

Copyright © Pearson Education, Inc., or its affiliates. All Rights Reserved.

Teaching Note: Read the prompt. Talk about why friends may need to make a decision, such as choosing an activity. Then review ways friends may make a decision about taking turns and sharing. Encourage the child to describe his or her final picture.

Collaboration and Creativity: Problem Solving

1. **Name** the problem.

2. **Think** of ways to solve it.

3. **Decide** the best way to solve the problem.

Copyright © Pearson Education, Inc., or its affiliates. All Rights Reserved.

Teaching Note: Read aloud the first step. Discuss the problem in the picture. Then read the second step and discuss the three ways the problem might be solved. Ask the child to choose what he or she thinks is the best way and tell why it is a good choice.

Try it!

1. Name the problem.

2. Circle the best way to solve the problem.

Copyright © Pearson Education, Inc., or its affiliates. All Rights Reserved.

Teaching Note: Point to the picture on the left, and ask children to tell you what they think the problem is. Then discuss the three possible solutions pictured. Ask the child which is the fairest way to solve the problem so that everyone can do an activity.

What are our country's symbols?

These symbols stand for the United States.

Copyright © Pearson Education, Inc., or its affiliates. All Rights Reserved.

Teaching Note: Explain that a symbol is something that stands for something else. Read the text aloud and identify the three symbols pictured. Discuss how the American flag, bald eagle, and Statue of Liberty are symbols of the United States.

What are our country's symbols?

Check the symbols that stand for the United States.

Copyright © Pearson Education, Inc., or its affiliates. All Rights Reserved.

Teaching Note: Read the prompt aloud. Point out the white box by each picture as the place to make a checkmark. When the child has completed the activity, ask which symbol for the United States he or she likes best and why.

What are our country's monuments?

These monuments remind us of important people.

Copyright © Pearson Education, Inc., or its affiliates. All Rights Reserved.

Teaching Note: Explain that a monument can be a building, a statue, or other structure that honors an important person. Discuss each monument pictured (Lincoln Memorial, the White House, Washington Monument) and who it honors.

23

What are our country's monuments?

Circle the place where our president lives and works.

Copyright © Pearson Education, Inc., or its affiliates. All Rights Reserved.

Teaching Note: Read the prompt aloud. Refer the child to the first page of the lesson for help if necessary. Then ask the child to describe the place where the president lives and works.

my Story Book

Draw people working together to do a job.

Copyright © Pearson Education, Inc., or its affiliates. All Rights Reserved.

Teaching Note: Read the prompt aloud. Talk about different jobs that people do by working together. Help the child identify a home, school, or community job that people might work together to do. Ask the child to tell about his or her finished drawing.

Copyright © Pearson Education, Inc., or its affiliates. All Rights Reserved.

Copyright © Pearson Education, Inc., or its affiliates. All Rights Reserved.

Chapter 2

Everybody Works

How do people get what they need?

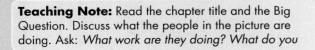

Teaching Note: Read the chapter title and the Big Question. Discuss what the people in the picture are doing. Ask: *What work are they doing? What do you think they will do with the tomatoes? Is food something that everybody needs? How do you know?*

Everybody Works

my Story Spark

Draw a picture of a job you do at home.

Copyright © Pearson Education, Inc., or its affiliates. All Rights Reserved.

Teaching Note: Read the prompt aloud. Brainstorm jobs children do at home. Ask the child to tell you what job he or she likes to do or would like to do at home. Have the child describe the finished drawing.

Begin With a Song

Lots of Jobs

Sing to the tune of "Skip to My Lou."

Baker, teacher,
doctor, too.

Lots of jobs
I'd like to do.

Care for animals
in the zoo.

What kinds of work
would you do?

Copyright © Pearson Education, Inc., or its affiliates. All Rights Reserved.

Teaching Note: Sing the song with the child as you point to the pictures. Help the child identify the tools used by a baker, a teacher, and a doctor; then the hats used by a cowboy, a firefighter, and a construction worker. Last, discuss what the zookeeper is doing.

Vocabulary Preview

Circle examples of these words in the picture.

needs

wants

money

job

goods

services

Copyright © Pearson Education, Inc., or its affiliates. All Rights Reserved.

Teaching Note: Point to each photo and then read the word aloud. Use the photo to talk about what the word means. Ask the child to describe what he or she sees in the central picture. Then assist him or her in circling an example of each word in the picture.

What do we need? What do we want?

Needs are things we must have to live.

needs

Wants are things we like to have.

wants

Copyright © Pearson Education, Inc., or its affiliates. All Rights Reserved.

Teaching Note: Read the text. Identify *needs* as clothing, food, and shelter. Identify *wants* as things we like but don't need. Help the child distinguish needs from wants. Discuss that people can want what they need when they choose food, clothing, and shelter they like.

What do we need? What do we want?

Draw lines to match each word with a picture.

1.

Need

Want

2.

Need

Want

Copyright © Pearson Education, Inc., or its affiliates. All Rights Reserved.

Teaching Note: Read the prompt aloud. Help the child read each word and identify each photo. Ask: *What picture shows something you need to live? What picture shows something you may like and want, but don't need to live?*

How do we get what we need or want?

We can trade.

We can buy and sell.

Copyright © Pearson Education, Inc., or its affiliates. All Rights Reserved.

Teaching Note: Talk about what people can do to get what they need or want. Ask the child if he or she has traded things with a friend. Discuss using money as a trade to buy things and receiving money from selling things.

How do we get what we need or want?

Finish the drawing. **Show** how they trade or sell.

Copyright © Pearson Education, Inc., or its affiliates. All Rights Reserved.

Teaching Note: Read the prompt aloud, and brainstorm examples of things that the children might trade or sell that would fit in the picture. Then have the child complete the activity. Talk about the finished picture.

How do we use money?

We use money to buy things we need and want.

Copyright © Pearson Education, Inc., or its affiliates. All Rights Reserved.

Teaching Note: Point to the picture on the left and help the child identify the one dollar bill and each coin. Then discuss the picture on the right. Talk about how the boy gets the lemonade he wants and what the girls might do with the money they earn.

How do we use money?

Circle what you can buy with money.

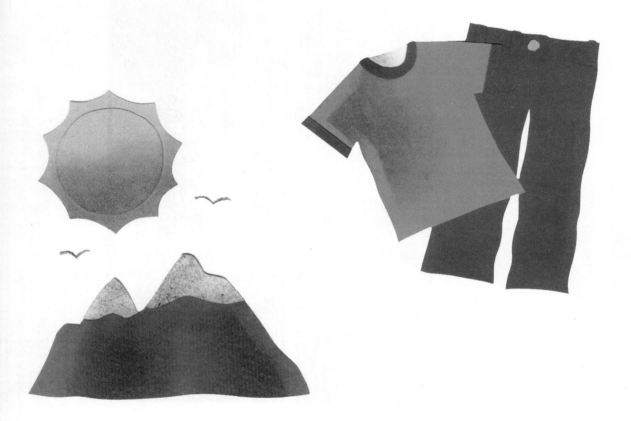

DINOSAURS

Copyright © Pearson Education, Inc., or its affiliates. All Rights Reserved.

Teaching Note: Read the prompt aloud. Discuss what each picture shows, and have the child complete the activity. Then talk about how money can be used to buy clothing and a book, but not the sun or a mountain.

Look and listen when a friend speaks. **Talk** clearly when you speak.

Copyright © Pearson Education, Inc., or its affiliates. All Rights Reserved.

Teaching Note: Read the text aloud. Practice listening and speaking by talking with the child about the job each child in the photo portrays. Ask the child which job he or she would like to do some day and why.

Collaboration and Creativity: Listening and Speaking

Try it!

Draw something you would like to buy. **Tell** a friend why.
Then **listen** to your friend.

Copyright © Pearson Education, Inc., or its affiliates. All Rights Reserved.

Teaching Note: Read the prompts aloud. If possible, have the child work with a partner to complete the activity. Be sure each child gets a turn to speak and a turn to listen. If a partner is not available, talk with the child about his or her drawing.

Copyright © Pearson Education, Inc., or its affiliates. All Rights Reserved.

Lesson 4
What are jobs that people do?

People do many kinds of jobs.

home

school

community

Teaching Note: Explain that a job is work that a person may do to earn money or as an unpaid volunteer to help others. Talk about the different jobs people do at home, in your school, and in your community. Ask the child what her or his favorite home job is.

39

What are jobs that people do?

Draw lines to match the workers with their tools.

Teaching Note: Read the prompt aloud. Brainstorm jobs and the tools needed for each. Then help the child identify each worker on the page and the tool the worker would need to do his or her job. Talk about what the workers do with their tools.

Copyright © Pearson Education, Inc., or its affiliates. All Rights Reserved.

Reading Skills: Cause and Effect

Ⓒ **RI.K.3.** Describe connection between two events in a text.

A cause is what makes something happen.

An effect is what happens.

cause

effect

Copyright © Pearson Education, Inc., or its affiliates. All Rights Reserved.

Teaching Note: Help the child learn *cause* and *effect* by using examples from the school day. Then discuss what the pictures show. Ask what the girl was paid to do. Explain that earning money was the effect of raking leaves, and that raking leaves caused the girl to earn money.

Reading Skills: Cause and Effect

Try it!

Look at the pictures. **Write C** on the cause. **Write E** on the effect.

Copyright © Pearson Education, Inc., or its affiliates. All Rights Reserved.

Teaching Note: Read the prompts aloud. Discuss what each picture shows. Ask: *What is the effect of the cat pushing the vase? What caused the vase of flowers to fall to the floor and break?* Assist the child in writing "C" and "E" on the correct picture.

Why do we make choices?

We can not have everything we want. We must make choices.

Copyright © Pearson Education, Inc., or its affiliates. All Rights Reserved.

Teaching Note: Read the text aloud and identify the photos. Then have the child recall a choice he or she made between two things. Ask: *What do you think about* *when you make a choice between two things?* Talk about why choices are necessary.

43

Why do we make choices?

What would you choose if you could buy only one?
Circle the picture. **Tell** why.

Copyright © Pearson Education, Inc., or its affiliates. All Rights Reserved.

Teaching Note: Read the prompt aloud. Discuss why we need to choose things and cannot just buy everything we want. Then have the child choose one thing to circle. Talk about why the child made that choice.

What are goods and services?

Goods are things people grow or make.

Services are work people do to help others.

Copyright © Pearson Education, Inc., or its affiliates. All Rights Reserved.

Teaching Note: Read the text aloud. Help the child identify the goods in the left photo and the service in the right photo. Discuss other goods people grow or make, using classroom or home examples. Then talk about different service jobs in your community.

What are goods and services?

Write G on pictures that show goods.
Write S on pictures that show services.

Copyright © Pearson Education, Inc., or its affiliates. All Rights Reserved.

Teaching Note: Write the letters "G" and "S", and have the child copy them on a sheet of paper. Then read the prompts aloud. Help the child identify which photos show goods and which show services. Assist the child in writing "G" or "S" on each photo.

my Story Book

Draw a picture of a job you would like. Show what you would make or do for others.

Copyright © Pearson Education, Inc., or its affiliates. All Rights Reserved.

Teaching Note: Read the prompts aloud. Review and discuss the different types of jobs from the chapter. Then assist the child as he or she completes the activity. When the drawing is finished, ask: *Does your picture show goods or a service?*

Copyright © Pearson Education, Inc., or its affiliates. All Rights Reserved.

Copyright © Pearson Education, Inc., or its affiliates. All Rights Reserved.

Chapter 3

Where We Live

 What is the world like?

Teaching Note: Read the chapter title and the Big Question. Discuss what the world in the photo is like. Help the child identify what he or she sees in the photo. Ask: *What do you think the weather is like? Does it look hot or cold here? How do you know?*

49

Where We Live

my Story Spark

Look out the window. **Draw** what you see.

Copyright © Pearson Education, Inc., or its affiliates. All Rights Reserved.

Teaching Note: Read the prompt aloud. Encourage the child to look out a nearby window and focus on details in his or her drawing. Ask the child to describe the drawing and show you from the window which object he or she chose to draw.

Begin With a Song

This Is My Community

Sing to the tune of "Twinkle, Twinkle, Little Star."

This is where I live and play,
work and shop most every day.

Here's my home and here's my street.
This is where my neighbors meet.

Lots of people live near me.
This is my community!

Copyright © Pearson Education, Inc., or its affiliates. All Rights Reserved.

Teaching Note: Review the meaning of community. Then sing the song as you point to each picture. Invite the child to sing with you. Discuss the features of your community and what the child might see if he or she took a walk with you.

map

hill

mountain

plain

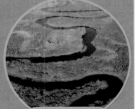

river

lake

Circle examples of these words in the picture.

Copyright © Pearson Education, Inc., or its affiliates. All Rights Reserved.

Teaching Note: Read each word aloud as you point to the photo. Talk about the meaning of each word. Then ask the child to describe what he or she sees in the central picture. Assist him or her in circling an example of each word in the picture.

Copyright © Pearson Education, Inc., or its affiliates. All Rights Reserved.

Lesson 1
Where do we live?

We live in neighborhoods.

Teaching Note: Define a neighborhood as the small area in which a person lives. Help the child identify the neighborhood place in each picture. Then discuss places the child may be familiar with in your school or home neighborhood.

Where do we live?

Draw a line from each place to something you see there.

Copyright © Pearson Education, Inc., or its affiliates. All Rights Reserved.

Teaching Note: Read the prompt aloud. Review the neighborhood places pictured. Brainstorm some things that might be seen in each place. Then have the child complete the activity by matching each item to a place.

Where are places located?

Some places are near. Some places are far.

My house is **behind** the park.

My house is **near** the school.

The hospital is on the **left**.

Copyright © Pearson Education, Inc., or its affiliates. All Rights Reserved.

Teaching Note: Discuss the model neighborhood shown in the photo. Note where each child is pointing and read aloud the text. Then talk about the location words the children use. Brainstorm additional words such as *above*, *below*, *behind*, and *in front*.

Lesson 2

Where are places located?

Think of two places in your neighborhood.
Draw them on the right and left of the library. **Label** each place.

library

Teaching Note: Discuss the places that are in your immediate school or home neighborhood, and make a list for the child to see. Read aloud the list and encourage him or her to use it to draw two places. Ask the child to describe the completed drawings.

56

Copyright © Pearson Education, Inc., or its affiliates. All Rights Reserved.

What do maps show?

Maps show real places. They can show big places or small places. They can show land and water.

Copyright © Pearson Education, Inc., or its affiliates. All Rights Reserved.

Teaching Note: Read the text aloud. Explain that the left map shows a big place, our country, and the right map shows a small place, a neighborhood. Help the child identify the land and water on both maps. Then point out your state on the U.S. map.

What do maps show?

Circle the teacher's desk on the map.
Draw a place where children can read books.

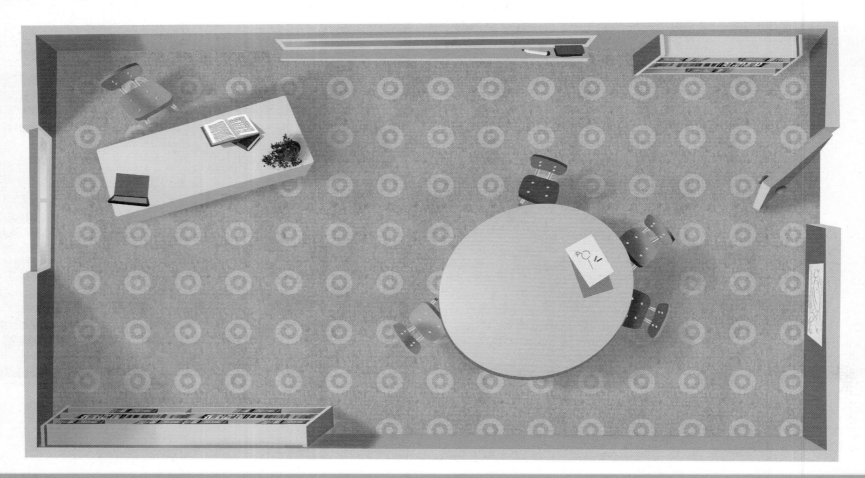

Copyright © Pearson Education, Inc., or its affiliates. All Rights Reserved.

Teaching Note: Explain that the map shows a view of a classroom from above. Help the child identify what is shown on the map. Then read the prompts aloud, and have the child complete the activity. Ask the child to describe his or her drawing.

Map Skills: Cardinal Directions

Directions tell us which way to go. Maps use **north**, **south**, **east**, and **west**. Look at the arrow that says north. The park is to the north.

Copyright © Pearson Education, Inc., or its affiliates. All Rights Reserved.

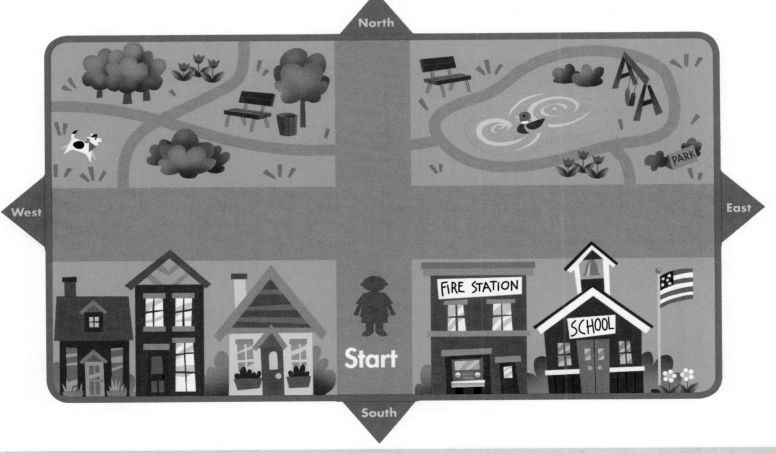

Teaching Note: Read the text aloud. Say each direction word as you point to the appropriate arrow on the map. Have the child put a finger on "Start" and move it up to the park, to the left to the dog, to the right to the pond, and down to the fire station. Say each direction as the child moves.

Map Skills: Cardinal Directions

Try it!

Put your finger on Start. **Choose** a direction.
Draw a line in that direction. **Tell** what you see there.

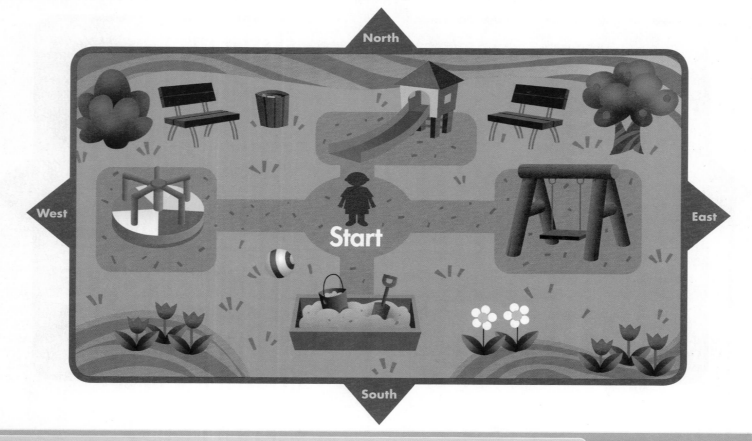

Copyright © Pearson Education, Inc., or its affiliates. All Rights Reserved.

Teaching Note: Review the direction words on the map. Then show the child where to place his or her finger to start. After the child draws a line, ask: *What direction did you choose? What do you see in that direction?*

What are landforms?

There are different kinds of land.

mountain

hill

North Carolina

North

West

East

South

Kentucky

West Virginia

Virginia

Tennessee

MOUNTAINS

HILLS

PLAINS

ISLANDS

Georgia

South Carolina

ATLANTIC OCEAN

plain

island

Copyright © Pearson Education, Inc., or its affiliates. All Rights Reserved.

Teaching Note: Discuss the photos and the names of the landforms. Then have the child use a finger to trace each line from a photo to the map. Talk about how the different landforms are pictured in symbols and colors on the map.

What are landforms?

Look at the map. **Circle** the mountains 🏔 and hills 🦫 .
Draw an X on the plains 🌾 and islands 🏝 .

Key
- mountains
- hills
- plains
- islands

Copyright © Pearson Education, Inc., or its affiliates. All Rights Reserved.

Teaching Note: Explain that the same map on the first page is shown here. Have the child match the landform symbols and colors in the directions and the key to those on the map. Then read the prompts aloud, and have the child complete the activity.

Copyright © Pearson Education, Inc., or its affiliates. All Rights Reserved.

Lesson 5
What are bodies of water?

There are different kinds of water.

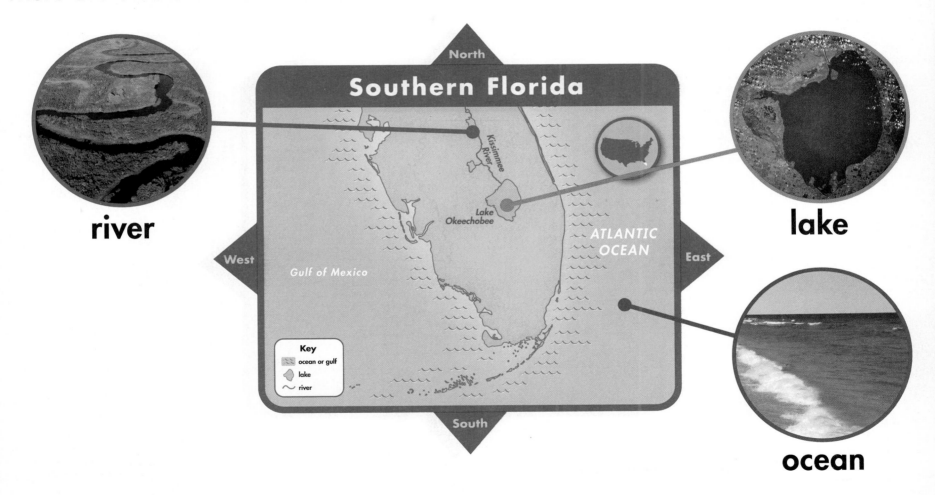

river

lake

ocean

Southern Florida

North

Kissimmee River

Lake Okeechobee

ATLANTIC OCEAN

West

East

Gulf of Mexico

South

Key
- ocean or gulf
- lake
- ~ river

Teaching Note: Name each body of water and discuss what is shown in the photo. Have the child trace each line from a photo to the map. Talk about how each kind of water is shown as a symbol and the color blue on the map and in the key.

What are bodies of water?

Write W on the water.

North

Louisiana

Key
gulf
lake
river

West

East

Mississippi River

Lake Pontchartrain

Gulf of Mexico

South

Copyright © Pearson Education, Inc., or its affiliates. All Rights Reserved.

Teaching Note: Write the word *Water* and point out the letter "W." Help the child write the letter on a separate sheet of paper. Then have the child look at the map and find the different kinds of water shown in blue. Assist the child in writing "W" on the water.

RI.K.3. Describe connection between two pieces of information in a text.

Reading Skills: Classify and Categorize

You can put things into groups when they are alike.

A hill and a mountain are landforms.

A river and an ocean are bodies of water.

Copyright © Pearson Education, Inc., or its affiliates. All Rights Reserved.

Teaching Note: Review the names for different landforms and bodies of water the child has learned. Explain that these names can be grouped as *land* or *water*. Then discuss what is shown in the *land* and *water* pictures.

© **RI.K.3.** Describe connection between two pieces of information in a text.

Try it!

Circle in brown the pictures that show kinds of land.
Circle in blue the pictures that show kinds of water.

Copyright © Pearson Education, Inc., or its affiliates. All Rights Reserved.

Teaching Note: Provide the child with a blue crayon and a brown crayon. Discuss what is shown in each photo. Then read aloud the prompts, and have the child complete the activity. Assist as needed.

What do globes show?

A globe is a model of Earth. It shows land and water.

Copyright © Pearson Education, Inc., or its affiliates. All Rights Reserved.

Teaching Note: If you have a globe, allow the child to examine it. Ask: *How is a globe a model of Earth?* To answer the question, discuss the globe's shape and what it shows. Have the child point to land and water on the globe.

What do globes show?

Color the water blue.
Color the land green.

Copyright © Pearson Education, Inc., or its affiliates. All Rights Reserved.

Teaching Note: Point to the illustrations. Explain that each globe shows a different side of the earth. Compare the illustrations with the photo on the previous page. Then provide a blue crayon and a green crayon, and have the child color the land and water.

Copyright © Pearson Education, Inc., or its affiliates. All Rights Reserved.

Lesson 7

What is weather like?

Weather can change.

rainy

cold

hot

Teaching Note: Explain what weather is. Talk about what the weather is like outside today. Ask the child to describe each photo. Then read each weather word aloud. Ask: *What is your favorite kind of weather?*

What is weather like?

Look at each kind of weather. **Draw** a line to what you would wear.

Copyright © Pearson Education, Inc., or its affiliates. All Rights Reserved.

Teaching Note: Use weather words from the previous page to talk about each scene at the top. Discuss the items shown in each picture at the bottom. Ask: *What do people wear in hot (cold, rainy) weather?* Read the prompts, and have the child complete the activity.

What are the seasons?

There are four seasons.

spring

summer

fall

winter

Copyright © Pearson Education, Inc., or its affiliates. All Rights Reserved.

Teaching Note: Read the text aloud. Then name the season with the child as you point to each picture. Discuss the weather shown in each picture. Focus on how the tree changes in each season. Ask: *What is your favorite season? Why?*

What are the seasons?

Choose a season.
Draw things on and around the tree that show your season.

Copyright © Pearson Education, Inc., or its affiliates. All Rights Reserved.

Teaching Note: Read the prompts aloud. Discuss what each of the four seasons is like and what the tree might look like in each season. Have the child complete the activity, and then describe the finished drawing by naming each item and how it relates to the season.

Copyright © Pearson Education, Inc., or its affiliates. All Rights Reserved.

Lesson 9
How do we use Earth's resources?

We use Earth's resources to meet our needs.

Teaching Note: Point to each photo at the top. Explain what resource is shown. Then follow the arrow down to the photo below and explain how the resource is used to meet a need. Brainstorm additional resources from the earth and how we use them to meet our needs.

73

How do we use Earth's resources?

Circle in green Earth's resources. **Circle** in red things people use or make.

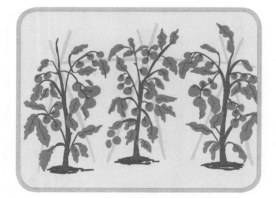

Teaching Note: Help the child identify what is shown in each picture. Provide a green crayon and a red crayon, and have the child complete the activity. Discuss the choices the child made.

Copyright © Pearson Education, Inc., or its affiliates. All Rights Reserved.

W.K.6. Explore digital tools for writing.

Copyright © Pearson Education, Inc., or its affiliates. All Rights Reserved.

my Story Book

Think of a place you would like to visit.
Draw a picture of what the place looks like.

Teaching Note: Read the prompt aloud. Brainstorm places and write them down. Then have the child complete the activity. Encourage the child to describe the completed drawing, and explain why he or she chose this place to picture.

Copyright © Pearson Education, Inc., or its affiliates. All Rights Reserved.

Our Traditions

Copyright © Pearson Education, Inc., or its affiliates. All Rights Reserved.

THE BIG ? How is culture shared?

Teaching Note: Explain that *culture* means "how a group of people live." Add that culture includes kinds of food, music, art, language, clothing, shelter, and celebrations. Discuss the Chinese New Year parade in the photo, and point out that the people are carrying a model of a Chinese dragon.

my Story Spark

Think of your favorite food. **Draw** a picture of it.

Copyright © Pearson Education, Inc., or its affiliates. All Rights Reserved.

Teaching Note: Read the prompt aloud. Brainstorm favorite foods with the child. After the drawing is completed, talk about what the child especially likes about the favorite food he or she drew. Ask about any special times when this food is served, such as for a celebration.

Begin With a Song

Holidays Are Special Days

Sing to the tune of "Yankee Doodle."

Holidays are special days

When families get together.

These are times we share good food

In any kind of weather!

There are times to have parades

Or have a celebration.

There are times to think about

Great people in our nation!

Copyright © Pearson Education, Inc., or its affiliates. All Rights Reserved.

Teaching Note: Sing the song together as you point to the picture that goes with each part. Then talk about the Fourth of July celebration shown in the last picture.

Explain that the figure is dressed as Uncle Sam, who is a symbol of our country. Ask the child to describe other celebrations.

Vocabulary Preview

Circle examples of these words in the picture.

family

custom

celebrate

holiday

tradition

culture

Copyright © Pearson Education, Inc., or its affiliates. All Rights Reserved.

Teaching Note: Discuss the Fourth of July parade shown in the central picture. Ask the child to identify Uncle Sam. Then point to and read aloud each word and discuss its meaning. Help the child look for and circle an example of each word in the picture.

How are people alike and different?

The children are alike, or the same. They are different, too.

Copyright © Pearson Education, Inc., or its affiliates. All Rights Reserved.

Teaching Note: Read the text aloud. Then discuss how the two children in the photo are alike and different. Ask the child to point out details such as the same ball, different colors, short sleeves versus long sleeves, and that both children are wearing glasses.

How are people alike and different?

Circle ways these sisters are alike.
Draw an X on ways they are different.

Copyright © Pearson Education, Inc., or its affiliates. All Rights Reserved.

Teaching Note: Read the prompts aloud. First talk about how the two girls shown are alike. Then discuss how they are different. Point out that two items that are alike, such as the shirts, can also be different, as in color. Then have the child complete the activity.

Copyright © Pearson Education, Inc., or its affiliates. All Rights Reserved.

Reading Skills: Compare and Contrast

© **RI.K.3.** Describe connection between two individuals or pieces of information in a text.

RI.K.9. Identify similarities/differences between two texts on same topic.

Some things are alike, or the same.
Other things are different, or not the same.

Teaching Note: Read aloud the text. Explain that *compare* means to see how the two photos are alike while *contrast* means to see how the two photos are different.

Discuss details of the two photos including the people and the activity shown. Talk about what is alike and different.

83

Reading Skills: Compare and Contrast

© **RI.K.3.** Describe connection between two individuals or pieces of information in a text.

RI.K.9. Identify similarities/differences between two texts on same topic.

Try *it!*

What do both pictures show?
Tell how they are alike and different.

Copyright © Pearson Education, Inc., or its affiliates. All Rights Reserved.

Teaching Note: Read the prompts aloud. Have the child tell you at least one example of a similarity and one example of a difference between the pictures. Then have the child complete the activity. Discuss what the child found when he or she is finished.

How are families alike and different?

Families can be large or small.

Copyright © Pearson Education, Inc., or its affiliates. All Rights Reserved.

Teaching Note: Have the child count the people in each photo and tell you if the family is large or small. Explain that families can include grandparents and other relatives, as well as one or more parents and children. Talk about how every family is different from yet similar to other families.

How are families alike and different?

Draw a picture of your family.

Copyright © Pearson Education, Inc., or its affiliates. All Rights Reserved.

Teaching Note: Read the prompt aloud. Review the names of immediate family members such as *mother*, *father*, *sister*, *brother*, *grandmother*, *grandfather*. After the drawing is finished, ask the child to describe what he or she drew. Make sure the child has included himself or herself in the picture.

What is culture?

We share ways to eat, dress, and have fun.

Copyright © Pearson Education, Inc., or its affiliates. All Rights Reserved.

Teaching Note: Read the text aloud. Then talk about what part of people's culture each photo shows. Discuss the different cultural items and celebrations the class has shared. Ask the child about cultural items and activities he or she shares with others.

What is culture?

Draw something that is part of your culture.

Copyright © Pearson Education, Inc., or its affiliates. All Rights Reserved.

Teaching Note: Read the prompt aloud. Review the different items and activities that are a part of culture. Then talk with the child about his or her culture. After the child has finished the drawing, discuss what is pictured and how it is a part of culture.

Copyright © Pearson Education, Inc., or its affiliates. All Rights Reserved.

Lesson 4

How do we celebrate?

We celebrate special days. We celebrate in many ways.

Teaching Note: Talk about the kinds of celebrations shown in the photos (quinceañera, graduation, wedding). Ask the child to describe celebrations or special days he or she has been a part of. Discuss the different ways people celebrate.

89

How do we celebrate?

Color what you use to celebrate.

Copyright © Pearson Education, Inc., or its affiliates. All Rights Reserved.

Teaching Note: Read the prompt aloud. Discuss the different items people use in celebrations, including flags, balloons, party hats, and special foods. Then have the child complete the activity. Ask him or her to name other celebration items that are not pictured.

Copyright © Pearson Education, Inc., or its affiliates. All Rights Reserved.

Lesson 5

What are national holidays?

We remember people and events when we celebrate holidays.

Teaching Note: Name some of the different national holidays that are celebrated in our country each year. Talk about the events and people that are remembered on those special days. Explain which holiday is represented in each photo on the page.

What are national holidays?

Draw a line to match each picture to a sentence.

We celebrate our country.

We remember our brave leaders.

We give thanks.

Copyright © Pearson Education, Inc., or its affiliates. All Rights Reserved.

Teaching Note: Talk about what the child sees in each picture and what holiday is represented. Then read each sentence aloud, and have the child match the sentence to a picture by drawing a line from the sentence to the picture.

Copyright © Pearson Education, Inc., or its affiliates. All Rights Reserved.

Lesson 6
Who are American folk heroes?

We tell stories about our country and people in the past.

Betsy Ross

Johnny Appleseed

John Henry

Paul Bunyan

Teaching Note: Explain that a folk hero is a real or make-believe person that people tell about in amazing stories. Point out that many of these heroes and stories come from different times in our country's history. Name each folk hero on the page and talk about his or her story.

Who are American folk heroes?

Circle the picture that stands for your favorite folk hero. Then **retell** the story.

Copyright © Pearson Education, Inc., or its affiliates. All Rights Reserved.

Teaching Note: Help the child name each item pictured and associate it with one of the folk heroes from the previous page. Then ask the child to pick an item that belongs to his or her favorite folk hero and retell the story heard from the first page. Ask why this folk hero is the child's favorite.

What are other cultures like?

There are many cultures around the world.

Copyright © Pearson Education, Inc., or its affiliates. All Rights Reserved.

Teaching Note: Talk about the different parts of culture that are shown in the photos, including music, food, clothing, shelter, and ways to cook and eat. Explain that these photos come from cultures in other countries, such as Peru and Italy.

What are other cultures like?

Color the things that you know.

Copyright © Pearson Education, Inc., or its affiliates. All Rights Reserved.

Teaching Note: Read the prompts aloud. Talk about the pictures, and make sure that the child can identify them. Use the photos on the first page of the lesson as a reference. Then have the child complete the activity. Ask what the child knows about the pictures he or she colored.

A fact is true. Fiction is made up.

Abraham Lincoln was a U.S. president.

fact

Jack climbed a giant beanstalk.

fiction

Copyright © Pearson Education, Inc., or its affiliates. All Rights Reserved.

Teaching Note: Read aloud the instructional text and then the examples of fact and fiction. Discuss the pictures as you encourage the child to look for factual and fictional details. Point out that beanstalks are real, but stalks as big as the one shown are make-believe.

Critical Thinking: Distinguish Fact From Fiction

Try it!

Circle the picture that shows a fact.

Paul Bunyan was as tall as a tree.

George Washington was our first president.

Teaching Note: Remind the child of the meaning of *fact* and *fiction*. Discuss what the pictures show and then read each sentence aloud. Have the child complete the activity and explain his or her picture choice.

Copyright © Pearson Education, Inc. or its affiliates. All Rights Reserved.

my Story Book

Think of something you celebrate.
Draw a picture of what you do.

Copyright © Pearson Education, Inc., or its affiliates. All Rights Reserved.

Teaching Note: Read the prompt aloud. Talk about the different celebrations shown in the lessons and also celebrations that the child knows. Ask the child to think of a celebration he or she is a part of and draw what happens at that event. Ask the child to describe his or her final picture.

Copyright © Pearson Education, Inc., or its affiliates. All Rights Reserved.

How does life change throughout history?

Copyright © Pearson Education, Inc., or its affiliates. All Rights Reserved.

Teaching Note: Read the chapter title and the Big Question. Talk about the meaning of *history* as "events that happen over time." Use the photos as examples of how children's dress and hairstyles have changed over time. Explain that every person has his or her own history.

Life Then and Now

my Story Spark

Draw a picture of yourself when you were little.
Then **draw** a picture of yourself now.

Copyright © Pearson Education, Inc., or its affiliates. All Rights Reserved.

Teaching Note: Read the prompts aloud. Ask the child to think about what he or she looked like as a baby and as a toddler. Discuss what has changed, such as height and type of clothes, and what has stayed the same, such as color of hair and eyes.

🎵 Begin With a Song

We Share History

Sing to the tune of "Twinkle, Twinkle, Little Star."

Study all your history.

Learn about the past with me.

Study customs of each kind.

Study artifacts you find.

Study landmarks everywhere.

History is what we share!

Copyright © Pearson Education, Inc., or its affiliates. All Rights Reserved.

Teaching Note: Sing the song as you point to the pictures. Review the meanings of *history* and *customs*. Explain that *artifacts* are things, such as tools and toys, that people make. Point out that old artifacts can be used to learn about history. Then sing the song together.

Vocabulary Preview

Circle examples of these words in the picture.

picture

calendar

timeline

OUR COMMUNITY

FEBRUARY

past

hero

community

Copyright © Pearson Education, Inc., or its affiliates. All Rights Reserved.

Teaching Note: Discuss the classroom scene shown in the central picture. Ask the child to point out and name objects. Then read each word aloud and talk about the photo. Help the child find and circle an example of each word in the picture.

Copyright © Pearson Education, Inc., or its affiliates. All Rights Reserved.

Lesson 1

What is my personal history?

History is the story of the past. We all have a history.

Teaching Note: Read the lesson title and the text. Explain that *personal* means "something that relates to a person." Discuss the kinds of events that are a part of everyone's personal history, such as the first day of school and learning to jump rope.

What is my personal history?

Circle in blue things you may have used as a baby.
Circle in red things you may use today.

Copyright © Pearson Education, Inc., or its affiliates. All Rights Reserved.

Teaching Note: Read the prompts aloud. Help the child identify the objects shown on the page. Discuss which things would be used by a baby and which by an older child. Then provide blue and red crayons, and have the child complete the activity. Discuss his or her choices.

© **RI.K.3.** Describe connection between two events in a text.

Reading Skills: Sequence

You can use **first**, **next**, and **last** to show the order of when things happen.

first

next

last

Copyright © Pearson Education, Inc., or its affiliates. All Rights Reserved.

Teaching Note: Read the text aloud. Then talk about the pictures. Ask: *What does the girl do first to get ready for school? What does she do next? What does she do last?* Help the child use *first, next,* and *last* to talk about the order of events in a school activity.

© **RI.K.3.** Describe connection between two events in a text.

Try it!

Look at the pictures.
Write first, next, or **last** under each picture to show the order.

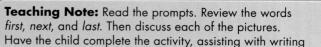

Copyright © Pearson Education, Inc., or its affiliates. All Rights Reserved.

Teaching Note: Read the prompts. Review the words *first, next,* and *last*. Then discuss each of the pictures. Have the child complete the activity, assisting with writing the words as necessary. Ask the child to share how he or she ordered the pictures.

Copyright © Pearson Education, Inc., or its affiliates. All Rights Reserved.

Lesson 2

How do we talk about time?

We can use **before**, **now**, and **after** to tell about time.

before

now

after

Teaching Note: Use the word *before*, *now*, or *after* to talk about each photo. Ask: *What happens before the children play music? What are the children doing now?* *What happens after the children play music?* Discuss the order of another classroom activity, using *before*, *now*, and *after*.

109

Look at each picture. **Draw** a picture to show what the girl would do after she paints.

before

now

after

Copyright © Pearson Education, Inc., or its affiliates. All Rights Reserved.

Teaching Note: Read the prompts, and discuss the two pictures that show the girl getting ready before she paints and getting a brush to start painting. Then have the child complete the activity. Ask the child to describe his or her completed drawing.

How do we measure time?

A calendar shows days of the week and months of the year.

SUNDAY	MONDAY	TUESDAY	WEDNESDAY	THURSDAY	FRIDAY	SATURDAY
	1	2	3	4	5	6
7	8	9	10	11	12	13
14	15	16	17	18	19	20
21	22	23	24	25	26	27
28	29	30				

NOVEMBER

Copyright © Pearson Education, Inc., or its affiliates. All Rights Reserved.

Teaching Note: Explain that the central picture is a calendar page for November. Read the names of the days and show that there are 30 days or 4 weeks and 3 days in the month. Discuss the two photos that illustrate November scenes.

How do we measure time?

Draw something you will do this month.

Copyright © Pearson Education, Inc., or its affiliates. All Rights Reserved.

Teaching Note: Read the prompt aloud. Help the child associate a month with each of the pictures on the page. Talk about the current month and what activities the child especially likes at this time. When the drawing is finished, ask the child to describe the activity he or she drew for the month.

Copyright © Pearson Education, Inc., or its affiliates. All Rights Reserved.

What is a timeline?

A timeline shows the order in which things happen.

1   2   3

Teaching Note: Trace the line from left to right with your finger. Explain that a timeline shows changes over time starting with the earliest picture on the left. Talk about how the chick grows and changes from hatching at number 1 to a young chick at number 2 to a full-grown chicken at number 3.

What is a timeline?

Show where the pictures go on the timeline.
Draw a line from each picture to a number.

1	2	3

Copyright © Pearson Education, Inc., or its affiliates. All Rights Reserved.

Teaching Note: Read the prompts aloud, and discuss the photos. Explain that two of the photos are out of order on the timeline. Have the child complete the activity. Then talk about what the child marked on the timeline for numbers 1, 2, and 3.

Copyright © Pearson Education, Inc., or its affiliates. All Rights Reserved.

Lesson 5

How can we learn about history?

We can listen to stories about the past.
We can look at pictures and things from the past.

Teaching Note: Review the meaning of *history*. Then talk about the ways to learn about the past depicted in each of the photos. Ask the child if he or she has viewed old photos, looked at old objects, or listened to family stories to learn about his or her history.

How can we learn about history?

Circle ways we can learn about history.

Copyright © Pearson Education, Inc., or its affiliates. All Rights Reserved.

Teaching Note: Read the prompts, and review the different ways to learn about history shown on the first page of the lesson. Then have the child complete the activity. Talk about the choices he or she circled.

Critical Thinking: Use Illustrations

Pictures can show what a sentence tells.

Jen washes her dog.

Copyright © Pearson Education, Inc., or its affiliates. All Rights Reserved.

Teaching Note: Read the instructional text aloud. Then discuss what is shown in the picture. Read aloud the sentence, and ask the child if it tells about the picture. Talk about how a picture can illustrate text and text can tell more about a picture.

Circle the picture that shows what the sentence says.

Matt feeds his fish.

Copyright © Pearson Education, Inc., or its affiliates. All Rights Reserved.

Teaching Note: Read the prompt and the sentence below the pictures. Make sure the child understands that he or she is to circle the picture that illustrates what the sentence says. Discuss why the other two pictures do not illustrate the sentence.

Who are American heroes from the past?

A hero works to help others.

Copyright © Pearson Education, Inc., or its affiliates. All Rights Reserved.

Teaching Note: Read the text aloud. Help the child identify the person in each picture. Then relate how each person helped others and discuss why we consider them heroes. Discuss other heroes from the past that the child has heard about.

Who are American heroes from the past?

Circle a picture of an American hero from the past. **Tell** the hero's story.

Copyright © Pearson Education, Inc., or its affiliates. All Rights Reserved.

Teaching Note: Point out to the child that the pictures on the page are the same people that were shown on the first page of the lesson. Have the child circle one picture and then help him or her retell that person's story. Ask why the child chose that particular person.

How have families changed?

Some things about families change. Some things stay the same.
Families wear different clothes. They do the same things in a new way.

then

now

Copyright © Pearson Education, Inc., or its affiliates. All Rights Reserved.

Teaching Note: Read the text aloud and discuss what the photos show. Talk about the differences and similarities the child sees between the "then" family and the "now" family. Help the child think of other ways families have changed and stayed the same from then to now.

How have families changed?

Draw lines from things used long ago to things we use today.

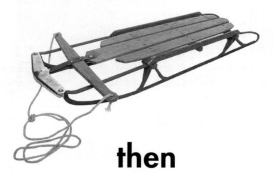

then   **now**

Copyright © Pearson Education, Inc., or its affiliates. All Rights Reserved.

Teaching Note: Read the prompt aloud, and help the child identify each picture on the page. Talk about the child's choices after he or she has completed the activity.

Ask: *How do you think clothing, cooking tools, and snow sleds might change in the future?*

How has school changed?

Some things about school change. Some things stay the same.
Children now sit in groups to read. They still put up a hand to speak.

then

now

Copyright © Pearson Education, Inc., or its affiliates. All Rights Reserved.

Teaching Note: Talk about the different ways that school has changed and stayed the same from the past to now. Use the photos and the words *then* and *now* to illustrate ideas. Also use examples in your classroom and from your own knowledge and experience.

How has school changed?

Circle things that were used in schools long ago.

Copyright © Pearson Education, Inc., or its affiliates. All Rights Reserved.

Teaching Note: Read the prompt aloud. Help the child describe each picture and complete the activity. Ask the child to explain his or her choices for things used long ago in schools. Talk about what it might have been like to write on a slate with chalk instead of using paper and pencil.

How have communities changed?

Some things about communities change. Some things stay the same. There are new buildings. Today people use cars.

then

now

Copyright © Pearson Education, Inc., or its affiliates. All Rights Reserved.

Teaching Note: Review the meaning of *community*. Then read the text aloud and discuss how communities can change and stay the same. Have the child compare the community in the "then" and "now" pictures and point out differences and similarities.

How have communities changed?

Look at the pictures of the same place then and now.
Circle what is different in the picture that shows now.

then

now

Copyright © Pearson Education, Inc., or its affiliates. All Rights Reserved.

Teaching Note: Read the prompt. Then have the child compare the two community pictures and circle the differences in the "now" picture. After the child is finished, discuss his or her choices. Compare the pictures and point out any additional differences.

Copyright © Pearson Education, Inc., or its affiliates. All Rights Reserved.

How has technology changed?

The tools and machines we use have changed from the past.

then

now

Teaching Note: Define *technology* as the tools and machines, such as computers, that people use to do their work. Read the text aloud and discuss the "then" and "now" photos. Help the child identify details in the photos, and talk about how office technology has changed.

How has technology changed?

Draw lines from things used in the past to things we use today.

then

now

Copyright © Pearson Education, Inc., or its affiliates. All Rights Reserved.

Teaching Note: Read the prompts. Discuss the pictures and make sure that the child recognizes each machine. Then have the child complete the activity. Talk about how the child marked the page. Ask: *Which things on the page have you seen or used?*

my Story Book

Draw one way people traveled long ago.
Then draw one way you travel today.

Copyright © Pearson Education, Inc., or its affiliates. All Rights Reserved.

Teaching Note: Read the prompts. Then brainstorm modes of transportation, past and present. List ideas under the labels of "Long Ago" and "Today." Then have the child complete the activity. After the drawing is finished, ask the child to describe his or her picture.

Copyright © Pearson Education, Inc., or its affiliates. All Rights Reserved.

Atlas

The United States of America, Political

CANADA

Washington

Montana

North Dakota

Minnesota

New Hampshire

Vermont

Maine

Oregon

Idaho

Wyoming

South Dakota

Wisconsin

Massachusetts

New York

Rhode Island

Connecticut

New Jersey

Nevada

Utah

Colorado

Nebraska

Iowa

Michigan

Pennsylvania

Delaware

Maryland

Washington, D.C.

California

Kansas

Missouri

Illinois

Indiana

Ohio

West Virginia

Virginia

Arizona

New Mexico

Oklahoma

Arkansas

Tennessee

Kentucky

North Carolina

South Carolina

ATLANTIC OCEAN

PACIFIC OCEAN

Texas

Mississippi

Alabama

Georgia

Louisiana

Florida

Alaska

MEXICO

Hawaii

Gulf of Mexico

Key

⭐ National Capital

Copyright © Pearson Education, Inc., or its affiliates. All Rights Reserved.

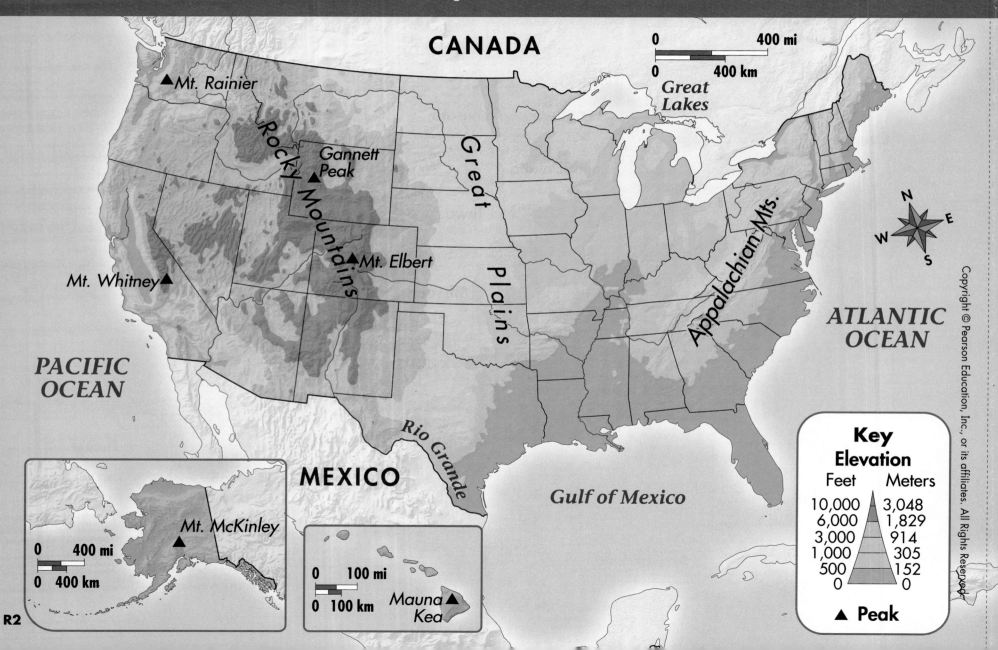

The United States of America, Physical

CANADA

Mt. Rainier

Rocky Mountains

Gannett Peak

Great Lakes

Great Plains

Mt. Elbert

Appalachian Mts.

Mt. Whitney

PACIFIC OCEAN

ATLANTIC OCEAN

Rio Grande

MEXICO

Gulf of Mexico

Mt. McKinley

0   400 mi
0   400 km

0   100 mi
0   100 km

Mauna Kea

0   400 mi
0   400 km

Copyright © Pearson Education, Inc., or its affiliates. All Rights Reserved.

Key
Elevation

Feet	Meters
10,000	3,048
6,000	1,829
3,000	914
1,000	305
500	152
0	0

▲ Peak

The World

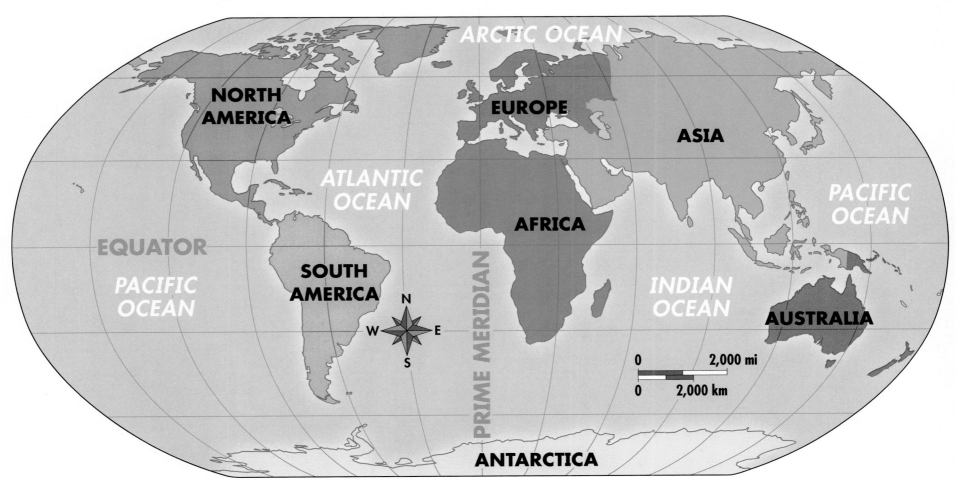

ARCTIC OCEAN

NORTH AMERICA

EUROPE

ASIA

ATLANTIC OCEAN

AFRICA

PACIFIC OCEAN

EQUATOR

PACIFIC OCEAN

SOUTH AMERICA

N
W E
S

PRIME MERIDIAN

INDIAN OCEAN

AUSTRALIA

0   2,000 mi
0   2,000 km

ANTARCTICA

Copyright © Pearson Education, Inc., or its affiliates. All Rights Reserved.